ECO-ACTION

Consumerism
of the Future

Angela Royston

Heinemann Library
Chicago, Illinois

Customer Service 888-454-2279
Visit our website at www.heinemannlibrary.com

Designed by Philippa Jenkins and Michelle
   Lisseter
Illustrations by Bridge Creative Services p. 8;
   Jeff Edwards p. 17; Philippa Jenkins pp. 12, 13
Printed and bound in China by South China
   Printing Co. Ltd.

12 11 10 09 08
10 9 8 7 6 5 4 3 2 1

**Library of Congress Cataloging-in-Publication
Data**
Royston, Angela.
   Consumerism of the future / Angela Royston.
      p. cm. -- (Eco-action)
Includes bibliographical references and index.
ISBN 978-1-4329-0128-8 (library binding -
hardcover) -- ISBN 978-1-4329-0133-2 (pbk.)
1. Consumption (Economics)--Environmental
aspects--Juvenile literature. 2. Consumer
behavior--Juvenile literature. 3. Consumer
behavior--Environmental aspects--Juvenile
literature. 4. Global warming--Juvenile literature.
I. Title.
HC79.C6R69 2008
339.4'7--dc22
                                  2007005807

Acknowledgments
The publishers would like to thank the following
for permission to reproduce photographs:
©Alamy pp. **35** (blickwinkel/Huetter), **14** (Brian
North), **23** (G. P. Bowater), **29** (mediacolor's),
43 (Melvyn Longhurst), **22** (Worldwide
Picture Library/Sue Cunningham); ©Corbis
pp. **27** (Bill Stormont), **7** (Gideon Mendel),
32 (Louie Psihoyos), **20** (Macduff Everton);
©Dreamstime.com pp. **21** (Alexander Ivanov),
18 (Elena Elisseeva), **4** (Heng Kong Chen), **19**
(Lockstockbob), **28** (Peter Pomorski), **37** (Yana
Petruseva); ©FLPA pp. **25** (Inga Spence), **24**
(Nigel Cattlin); ©Getty Images pp. **6** (AFP/STR),
5 (Stone/Jaime Villaseca), **38** (Stone/Philip &
Karen Smith); ©Harcourt Education Ltd pp. **11**,
30, **33** (Tudor Photography); ©istockphoto.com
pp. **41** (Arthur Kwiatkowsk), **42** (Todd Smith);
©NHPA p. **9** (Bill Coster); ©Photolibrary p. **17**
(Maximilian Stock Ltd); ©Still Pictures pp. **31**
(argus/Peter Frischmuth), **39** (Jorgen Schytte),
26 (Nick Cobbing), **36** (Peter Hirth), **34** (Roger
Braithwaite), **15** (Ron Giling), **10** (ullstein – Oed).

Cover photograph of fresh apples, variety Jazz,
reproduced with permission of Photolibrary.

Every effort has been made to contact copyright
holders of any material reproduced in this book.
Any omissions will be rectified in subsequent
printings if notice is given to the publishers.

Contents

Any words appearing in the text in bold, **like this**, are explained in the Glossary.

Shopping Bonanza

Consumers in North America, Europe, Japan, and Australia are enjoying a shopping bonanza. Racks of cheap clothes, computers, DVD players, CD players, and televisions fill our stores. Many people change their cell phones every year, and supermarket shelves are crammed with every kind of food all year round. The range of goods becomes wider and their prices ever cheaper.

Cheap and cheerful

The cheaper goods become, the more people in **developed countries** buy. The companies who manufacture the goods are often very large. They carry out their operations around the world and spend huge sums of money on advertising and marketing to persuade people that buying their goods will make them happy.

Who pays the price?

The majority of people in the countries where many of the goods are manufactured do not share this shopping bonanza. Most goods are made in China, India, Pakistan, and countries in Southeast Asia and Latin America and then transported to other countries around the world. The goods are cheap because the workers in these countries are paid very low wages—so low that sometimes children have to work so their families can survive.

Shopping malls are crammed with cheap goods.

Earth's resources

Electronic and many other goods are made mostly from metals and other materials found in the ground. Plastic and other **synthetic materials**, for example, are made from oil. These materials are all part of Earth's resources. Some materials are plentiful, but others are in short supply.

Factories use machinery that runs on electricity to manufacture goods. The electricity is generated in power stations, usually by burning coal, oil, or natural gas. These are called **fossil fuels**, and they are part of Earth's resources, too. So, consumerism, meaning the production and sale of more and more goods, is using up more and more of Earth's resources. It is also causing an even bigger problem—**global warming**.

This mine in Zambia, in Africa, extracts copper that is sold to companies in the West.

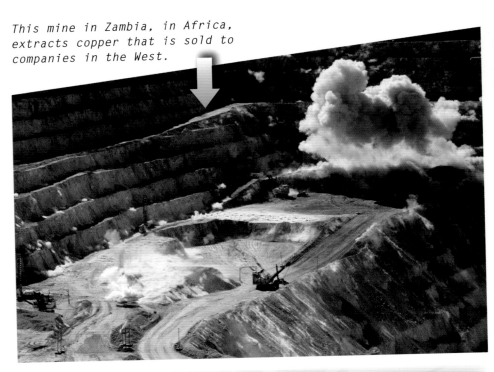

EXPLOIT OR CONSERVE?

Many companies and governments act as though Earth's resources are there for them to exploit as they like. Other people think Earth's resources should be used carefully and preserved for future generations. Do you think the way companies use resources and treat people in other countries should be more strictly **regulated**?

Hidden Costs

The way that most companies and most farmers produce goods and food is wasting Earth's resources and contributing to the greatest problem of all— global warming. The temperature of Earth is becoming warmer, and this is causing climates around the world to change more rapidly than ever before. Global warming and **climate change** threaten the world with catastrophes that could kill millions of people and make life very difficult for billions more.

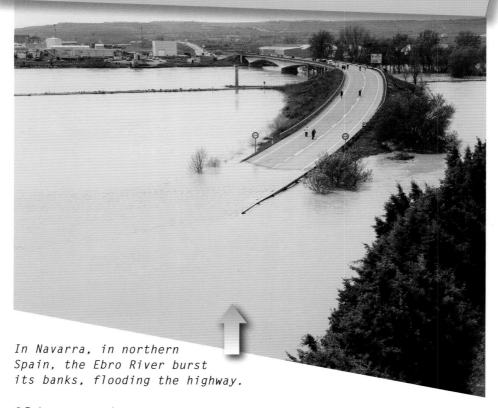

In Navarra, in northern Spain, the Ebro River burst its banks, flooding the highway.

Climate change

As the world gets warmer, **droughts** will become more common in many parts of the world. Deserts such as the Sahara, which is already spreading farther south into Africa, will spread even faster. Droughts cause people's food crops to fail and their cattle to die, creating famine and making people more likely to succumb to disease.

Climate change will bring more extreme weather. Heavy rain in some areas will cause rivers to rise, flooding large areas of farmland. Severe **hurricanes** and **typhoons** will become more common. The year 2005 was a particularly bad year for hurricanes, with many storms, including Hurricane Katrina, battering the southern coast of the United States and the islands of the Caribbean. Storms like these can kill people and cause millions of dollars worth of damage.

Long-term effects

The long-term effects of global warming are even more serious. As temperatures rise worldwide, thick ice in the Arctic and Antarctic will begin to melt. When land ice melts, extra water pours into the world's oceans, causing the sea level to rise. As sea levels rise, low-lying coastal areas will be flooded. If we do not act to reduce and stop global warming, even cities such as New York and London will eventually be flooded.

Changes in climate have happened before, but they have occurred over thousands of years. People can adapt to climate change—if they have time. But today, Earth is warming so fast there is not enough time for most people and countries to prepare for it.

WHO SHOULD TAKE RESPONSIBILITY?

The people who will suffer the most from climate change are the world's poorest people. They are the ones for whom drought, disease, and flooding will be most severe, and they are the ones who can least afford to cope with these catastrophes. Climate change is caused mainly by the way developed countries use Earth's resources and burn fossil fuels. Should people in these countries take responsibility for their actions? If so, we must change the way we live to avoid the worst effects of climate change.

In 2006 a severe drought in East Africa killed thousands of cattle, destroying the main source of local people's food.

Living in a greenhouse

How does mining Earth's resources and burning fossil fuels cause global warming? The answer lies in the gas **carbon dioxide** and certain other gases that are produced when fossil fuels are burned. They are also produced during some industrial processes. Carbon dioxide occurs naturally in the atmosphere. It is produced by living things as they breathe out and when they die. The bodies of living things are composed largely of carbon and, as they decompose or are burned, the carbon combines with oxygen in the air to make more carbon dioxide. This carbon dioxide is not the cause of the problem, however, because it is recycled by plants to make food in a process called **photosynthesis**. Global warming is caused by the billions of tons of additional carbon dioxide produced every year by burning fossil fuels.

The greenhouse effect

Carbon dioxide causes global warming because, like a greenhouse, it traps the Sun's heat. As the Sun's heat shines down, most of it is absorbed by the land and the sea, while the rest is reflected back into the atmosphere. The absorbed heat is then released and, as long as much of it escapes back into space, the temperature stays fairly even, making it possible for life to exist. Excess carbon dioxide in the air, however, is now trapping this released heat, making Earth warmer.

Carbon dioxide in the air stops heat from escaping. This warms the air below, acting like a greenhouse.

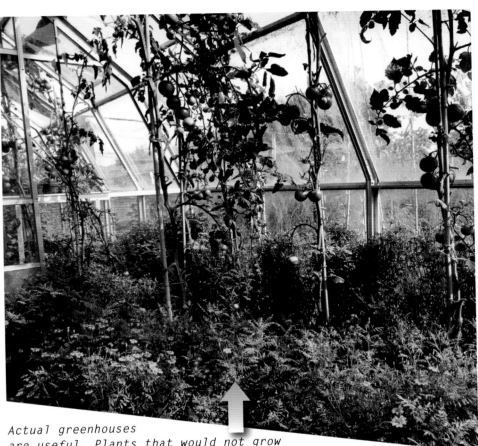

Actual greenhouses
are useful. Plants that would not grow
so well in the colder air outside grow in
the warmer air.

Why is global warming happening now?

For thousands of years, people produced very little extra carbon dioxide. They fertilized farm crops with animal manure and made many goods from wood. The population of the world was lower, and most people owned fewer clothes and other goods. They did not have electricity, motor vehicles, or airplanes, and they had not discovered how to turn oil into plastic and other synthetic materials. These discoveries have all come in the last 100 years and have transformed the way we live. But they have also led to the burning of billions of tons of fossil fuels and the addition of about 40 billion tons of extra carbon dioxide to the atmosphere each year.

Most power stations burn coal, oil, or gas to generate electricity. Factories, warehouses, and stores that make and sell consumer goods all use large amounts of electricity.

Fossil fuels

Fossil fuels formed millions of years ago from the remains of plants and animals. Coal formed from the remains of huge forests that grew about 300 million years ago, before the dinosaurs roamed Earth. Oil and natural gas formed from the remains of tiny marine organisms that lived even earlier.

Mining and drilling

People mine for coal. Machines cut coal from rocks, and the coal is taken, often in trains, to **power stations**. Here, it is burned, heating water to create steam. The steam turns **turbines**, and this generates electricity. Sometimes power stations buy coal from other countries, so the coal is transported hundreds or thousands of miles in ships and overland by road or rail.

Oil usually forms deep underground between layers of rocks. People drill through the rock to reach the oil and bring it to the surface. Some oil is pumped through pipes to an oil **refinery**, but much is carried by huge oil tankers that may sail halfway around the world.

Carbon dioxide is not the only **greenhouse gas**. Water vapor, **methane**, **nitrous oxide**, ozone, and **chlorofluorocarbons** (CFCs) are greenhouse gases, too. After water vapor, carbon dioxide is the most abundant. The oceans, tropical **rain forests**, and other carbon "sinks" can absorb about half of the carbon dioxide we produce at present, but the rest creates the greenhouse effect.

Refining oil

Once oil reaches a refinery, it is heated and separated into many different substances. Much of it is made into fuel for transportation— gasoline for road vehicles, diesel fuel for trucks, ships, and diesel trains, and kerosene for aircraft. Some of it is burned in power stations to generate electricity. The heaviest material is bitumen, a black tarry substance that is used on roads and roofs. The part of the oil that is made into gasoline is also made into plastics and different chemicals, such as those used in fertilizers. Polythene and acrylics are used to make cloth, paints, glues, toys, packaging, and many other things. The list of things that are made from oil is almost endless and includes some that might surprise you, such as medicines.

TOO VALUABLE TO BURN?

Because oil is the basis of so many materials that we now rely on, many people think that it is too precious to waste as fuel for transportation and for power stations. There are still large supplies of oil under the ground, but even if we burned a quarter of them, Earth would be subjected to irreversible, runaway global warming.

These are some of the many products made from oil.

How shopping contributes to global warming

Most consumer goods contribute to global warming at every stage of their production and distribution. Machines use energy to extract raw materials, and vehicles burn fossil fuel to transport them to factories. Factories use energy to manufacture and package the goods, and ships and trucks burn diesel fuel to take the finished goods to warehouses and stores. Finally, shoppers often drive to and from stores and shopping malls, burning gasoline in their cars.

From raw materials to finished goods

Most goods are made from materials that come from different parts of the world, and the finished goods are often sold worldwide. For example, the trees that were pulped to make the paper for this book grew in North America or in Scandinavia. The paper was then shipped to China, where it was printed and bound into books. The ink and glue were manufactured from oil and transported to the printer separately.

MAKING AND DISTRIBUTING A SINGLE CD

One Swedish musician, Eric Prydz, discovered that producing and distributing 40,000 CDs of his single "Proper Education" created 60.4 tons of carbon dioxide. The diagram to the left shows how much of this came from manufacturing the CD, promoting it, and distributing it. More than half the carbon dioxide was produced by the trucks that transported the CD to stores across the country.

video production, editing, staff, transportation

distribution

60% (36.3 tons)

10% (6.04 tons)

10% (6.04 tons)

20% (12.08 tons)

record company promotions and touring

manufacturing

Different stages of the production and distribution of a CD single contribute to a total of 60.4 tons of carbon dioxide.

The finished books were shipped to North American, Europe, and countries around the world. In fact, the book you are holding has probably traveled farther than most of its readers!

Unsustainable lifestyles

People in industrialized countries consume much more of Earth's resources per person than the rest of the world. It has been calculated that, if everyone in the world shared the same lifestyle as the average person in the United States, it would take over five planets like Earth to supply the resources needed. This is why people say that the way of life in developed countries is not sustainable. The following chapters look at different ways consumerism contributes to global warming and some of things we can do about it.

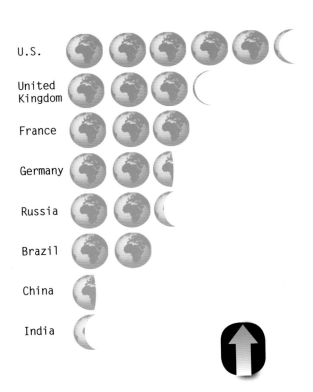

This diagram shows how many planet Earths it would take to provide the resources for everyone in the world to live like citizens of each of these countries.

Freight Miles

Very few of the consumer goods that shoppers buy in North America, Europe, or Australia are actually manufactured in any of these countries. The companies that design and sell them pay factories in countries such as China and Korea to make them, because wages there are lower. This means that raw materials and consumer goods are being shipped back and forth across the world, and every journey involves vehicles of some kind burning fossil fuels. Farm produce is also transported around the world, and this can create additional problems.

Cotton

Cotton is one of the most abundant crops grown in the southeastern United States, but very little cotton is made into clothes in the U.S. Instead, cotton that is grown in South Carolina may be shipped to Sudan in Africa to be spun and woven into cloth. Then, the cloth is sent to a factory in Pakistan to be made into garments. The garments are then shipped back to the United States and to other countries.

Flowers from abroad

How is it that you can buy roses and other flowers all year round in supermarkets? The answer is that they are flown in from hot countries, such as Kenya and Ecuador. The flowers are sent by **air freight** so that they do not wilt and die before they reach the customer.

Aircraft produce much more carbon dioxide than ships.

14

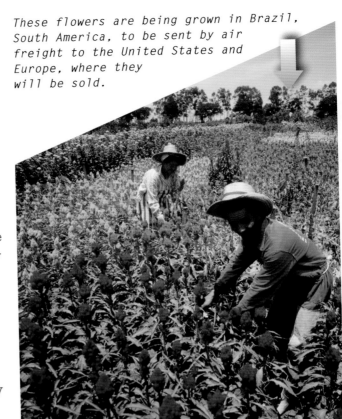

These flowers are being grown in Brazil, South America, to be sent by air freight to the United States and Europe, where they will be sold.

Using air freight is expensive, but the companies still make money because they pay the workers who grow and pick the flowers such low wages. And, by growing them in a country with a tropical climate, they can be grown and sold all year round.

Land and water

Importing flowers, fruits, and vegetables from abroad creates other problems. The flowers take up land that could be used to grow food for local people, and they can deprive local people of much-needed water. In parts of Kenya, farmers claim that they can no longer support their families because the companies that grow flowers are taking too much water from the Ngiro River, Kenya's second largest river.

Some companies in western countries have set up factories in **developing countries** to make soft drinks to sell in North America and Europe. The factories use so much water from underground supplies that the traditional wells have dried up. Similarly, Israeli and Egyptian farmers grow fruits and vegetables to sell in Europe, although both countries have limited supplies of water. The Israelis take large amounts of water from underground supplies that they share with neighboring countries and from the Jordan River, depriving local people of the water they need to grow food for themselves.

Food miles

Processed food contributes to global warming at almost every stage of its production, but particularly in transportation and distribution, which accounts for about half the total carbon dioxide produced by the food industry. Most processed food is made and packed in factories. The ingredients for ready-made meals, snacks, and other foods come from different places, often from different countries. Once the food is prepared, it is packed and transported to food depots, stores, and supermarkets. Customers often drive to and from stores and supermarkets.

The most extravagant form of transportation is air-freight. Tons of fruits and vegetables are flown around the world, producing more tons of carbon dioxide than the weight of the food itself. For example, pineapples sent from Hawaii to the U.S. mainland produce ten times their own weight of carbon dioxide.

INTERNATIONAL INGREDIENTS

A box of chocolates is one example of a product that uses ingredients that are shipped from many different countries. The countries given here are just a few of the possible sources:

- Chocolate, made from cocoa beans from West Africa or Central America
- Sugar from the Caribbean
- Almonds from Spain
- Coffee (in coffee cream) from Brazil
- Hazelnuts from Turkey
- Oranges (in orange cup) from Spain or the United States
- Vanilla from Tahiti

Tropical fruit is delicious, but is it worth damaging the planet to fly it to cooler countries?

Exotic fruits and vegetables

There are two main reasons why fruits and vegetables are flown to Europe, Japan, and North America. The first is to supply them with exotic tropical fruits that do not grow in their cooler climates. Fruits such as lychees, star fruit, and mangos are increasingly sent via air freight across the United States, from Hawaii to the mainland. But avoiding air miles does not mean that we have to give up eating fresh tropical fruit. For decades, bananas have been shipped to cooler countries from the Caribbean and Central America. The fruit is picked before it is ripe and slowly ripens on the ship. Ships carry much more produce and burn less fuel than aircraft.

Luxury foods

The second reason for sending items via air freight is to supply fresh fruits and vegetables out of season. When food is out of season in the northern hemisphere, it is brought in from the southern hemisphere. It often has to be sent by air, because it would rot if it came by ship. Fresh apricots, strawberries, and blueberries, for example, are flown to Europe from New Zealand. Some crops are imported even when they are in season.

When it is winter in the northern hemisphere, it is summer in the southern hemisphere. So, strawberries ripen in the north in June and in the south in December.

When you buy food directly from a farm, you know that it is fresh and in season.

Shopping solutions

Is there anything you can do to combat the excessive distances that many goods travel before they reach the stores? One thing you can do is to ask where fruits and vegetables come from, and try to choose things grown closest to you. You can also find out which foods are in season and which are produced locally.

Consumer choice

Fruits, vegetables, shellfish, and flowers are flown across the world to provide us with more choice, so the most effective thing to do is not to buy them. Supermarkets in particular pay a lot of attention to what customers say and what they do and do not buy. If the label on an item of food does not tell you which country it comes from, then ask one of the employees. Write to the company and tell them if you think they should not sell goods sent via air freight.

What is in season?

Food companies put a lot of effort into how food looks, but it is how it tastes that really matters. Fresh food tastes better, and locally grown food should be the freshest. If you are not sure what foods are in season, ask someone who grows food in their own garden. Most fruits ripen in the summer and early fall. Salad vegetables usually grow best in summer, but there are many vegetables that are in season in winter, including root vegetables and green vegetables such as winter kale.

Supermarkets now pay such low prices to farmers that more and more farmers are selling their produce direct to shoppers at farmers' markets. Local markets and farm stores are the best way of buying fresh, local food that is in season. Instead of having no link with the way the food was produced, you often buy it from the farmers themselves!

No choice

With many goods it is impossible to know how far the materials and ingredients have traveled before they get to you, and some goods are not available except as cheap imports. The outer layer of a soccer ball, for example, consists of several pieces sewn together by hand. It takes three hours and is often done by children in southern Asia. If a worker in the United States were paid to do this work, the ball would be many times more expensive.

One way to cut down on food miles is to grow some of your own food, such as this pot of basil.

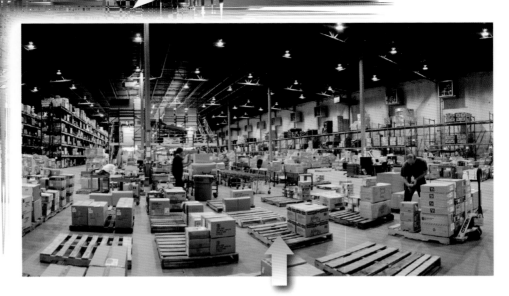

This warehouse stocks more books than any bookstore. It supplies people who order through the Internet.

FUTURISTIC OR FANTASY?

RepRap is an extraordinary invention developed by scientists at Bath University in Great Britain. The machine is like a three-dimensional printer. Instead of squirting ink from a nozzle, it squirts plastic to build copies of 3D shapes, such as toys. The inventors claim that RepRap will eventually be able to make almost everything. The instructions for the shapes would be bought or shared on the Internet. This would cut out the need not only for stores, but also for many factories, and so it would cut even more carbon **emissions**.

The end of stores?

The example of the amount of carbon dioxide created in the production and distribution of a CD (see page 12) showed that most was produced by transporting the CD to stores. But this did not include all the tons of carbon dioxide produced by the people who traveled to and from the store to buy the CD. Perhaps the answer is to get rid of stores. Sounds crazy? Maybe, but it is already beginning to happen.

Shopping from home

People already use alternative ways of shopping. You can buy almost everything through the Internet or from catalogs. Almost all major stores have websites where you can browse and buy what you want. Buying from catalogs and websites gives you the same guarantees that you would get from buying in a store, and the goods are delivered directly to your door. Television shopping channels also offer goods for sale.

Shopping from home certainly saves gasoline—or does it? One problem is that people are often not home when their packages are delivered, and so they have to travel to the sorting office to get them. Another problem is that small, independent stores lose the local customers they rely on. Shopping from stores you can walk to uses the least energy.

Superstores or warehouses?

Ecologist George Monbiot has suggested that superstores should become warehouses. Instead of thousands of people driving to a shopping mall, they would order what they wanted on the Internet and the goods would be delivered to them. Converting superstores to warehouses would save more than gasoline. Stores use huge amounts of energy in lighting, heating, and cooling. Supermarkets, for example, display many foods in open, cool cabinets. The cabinets keep the food fresh, but they cool the air in the store, too, which means that the heating has to be turned up even higher!

Goods ordered on the Internet are delivered to your door.

21

Fertilizers allow farmers to get better yields, but they add to global warming and can damage the environment.

Chemicals and factory farming

Today, most modern farms are run like factories. Chemical fertilizers allow farmers to grow the same crop on the same land, year after year. Growing just one crop is called **monoculture**, and it encourages pests that like to feed on it. Farmers kill the pests by spraying the crops with chemical pesticides. Producing chemicals consumes large amounts of energy. Animals are often reared indoors and fed with artificial feeds. This kind of farming, called **factory farming**, allows farmers to produce more food more cheaply, but it is one of the biggest contributors to global warming.

Farming with chemicals

Chemical fertilizers make plants grow even when the natural nutrients in the soil are exhausted. Chemical fertilizers, however, produce nitrous oxide, a greenhouse gas that traps 300 times more heat than the same weight of carbon dioxide. It takes much less nitrous oxide than carbon dioxide to increase global warming.

Insects, field mice, and other small animals feed on the same crops as we do. Farmers poison them with chemicals called pesticides. Diseases such as potato blight flourish in large areas of one crop. Farmers protect their crops by spraying them with more chemicals. Cotton is sprayed with more pesticides than any other crop.

Cotton-workers and people who live near cotton fields frequently suffer from pesticide poisoning. Apples are prone to several diseases and are sprayed up to seven times as they ripen on the trees. Some of the chemicals remain in the foods we eat and may damage our health.

Farm animals

Chickens and other farm animals do not escape chemicals. Instead of living outside, large factory farms keep huge amounts of animals indoors. Because the animals are crowded together, diseases easily take hold and spread. Farmers combat diseases by injecting the animals with **antibiotics** before they are even sick. Dairy cattle are also given large doses of **hormones** to make them produce more milk. We take in some of these antibiotics and hormones when we eat or drink the food.

GROWN OR MINED?

So much fossil fuel is used by the food industry that many ecologists now claim that our food is "mined," rather than grown. Farming is responsible for about one-quarter of the carbon dioxide emitted by the food industry. Farmers burn gasoline and diesel oil in tractors, sprayers, combine harvesters, and other farm machinery, while weed-killers, fertilizers, and pesticides are manufactured from oil using fossil fuels.

Growing cotton is sprayed up to 20 times with pesticides that damage the workers' health, too.

Many people in the United States and Europe are opposed to genetically modified food. These people are protesting.

Genetically modified

For hundreds of years, farmers have bred plants and animals to increase their yields. By carefully selecting, for example, which bulls to breed with which cows, they have produced cows that give more milk. This is called **selective breeding** because it selects particular characteristics. **Genetic modification**, however, introduces characteristics from one species into another. Ecologists say that genetic modification is not only unnatural, but it is also dangerous.

How does genetic modification work?

Breeding occurs when genes from a female unite with genes from a male to form a new and different individual. In nature, females can only breed with males of the same species. Scientists now, however, are able to add genes from one species to the genes of another species. They might, for example, introduce a gene from a different plant into tomato genes to make tomato plants that are resistant to a particular disease.

Problems with GM

The main argument against GM is that we do not know what the long-term effects of tampering with nature will be. For example, one company genetically modifies seeds so that they are resistant to a powerful **herbicide** that kills weeds. Some of these weeds, however, belong to the same species as the crop. This means that they can breed with the GM plants, producing superweeds that are also resistant to herbicides.

People are also concerned about the long-term effects on humans. With GM, it is impossible to know exactly what you are eating. Someone who has an allergy to nuts, for example, could eat wheat that includes genes from nuts and become sick.

Who will benefit?

GM companies claim that their products will save the world from famine, but most genetic modifications are aimed at consumers in developed countries, not at providing food for the poor. The seeds are expensive, and many GM seeds have to be used with a particular pesticide, which is an additional cost.

TERMINATOR SEEDS

Terminator seeds are one idea GM companies have for making money. Usually farmers save some seeds from their harvest to plant the following year, but terminator seeds do not produce fertile seeds. Instead, farmers would be forced to buy new seeds from the GM company every year—an extra cost for poor farmers. Ecologists say this is immoral. In 2007 the **United Nations** banned terminator seeds for the time being, but will the ban last?

Genetically modified crops are common in the United States. Food is produced from a mixture of non-GM crops and GM crops, so consumers do not know which they are eating.

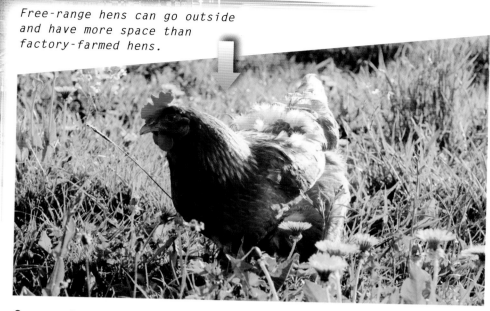

Free-range hens can go outside and have more space than factory-farmed hens.

Organic farming

Organic farming is really traditional farming. It uses farming methods developed over centuries to keep the soil and plants healthy. Organic farming avoids chemical fertilizers and pesticides and uses about one-quarter of the energy that modern farms use.

Traditional methods

In the past, farmers grew several different crops. They rotated them so that each field grew a different crop from the previous year. In this way, pests and diseases that target a particular crop did not become established. Every year one field would not be planted, and this gave the soil a chance to recover its nutrients. Organic farmers use this system of **crop rotation**. Instead of using chemical fertilizers that create huge amounts of nitrous oxide (see page 24), organic farmers use natural fertilizers, such as animal manure, and every three years they plant peas and other crops that fix nitrogen in the ground instead of releasing it into the air. Since plants grown organically are less prone to disease, they do not have to be sprayed in the same way **intensively produced crops** do.

Organic farms and farms that produce **free-range** meat allow their animals to go outside and live more natural lives, as they used to in the past. Free-range animals are healthier than factory-farmed animals and are not routinely given antibiotics.

Advantages

Free-range and organically farmed animals are treated more humanely than factory-farmed animals. Because the animals are free to move around and are fed a natural diet, many people think that the meat tastes better, too. Organic crops are free of poisonous sprays and are therefore healthier for us. More farmworkers are needed on organic farms, so it provides more jobs. This is particularly useful in developing countries.

Disadvantages

Plants grown organically do not produce as big a crop as plants grown using modern farming methods, and fruit often has more blemishes. Blemishes, however, only affect the way that something looks, not the way it tastes. More and more people are buying organic food—so many people, in fact, that local farms cannot supply enough. Instead, supermarkets buy much of their organic produce from abroad, thus adding to global warming by increasing freight miles.

CAN WE AFFORD CHEAP FOOD?

Organic food is often more expensive than non-organic food. Food produced using modern farming methods is cheap, but it damages the environment and produces tons of extra greenhouse gases. We do not pay for this damage in the price of the food, but we will pay for global warming in the future. Is the cost of cheap food worth it?

Although organic fruits and vegetables do not contain pesticides and other chemicals, you still have to wash them before you eat them.

Waste Mountain

Consumer goods are so cheap that people buy more and more, and many are wasted. Most people replace their cells phones every 18 months or so, throwing away the old one. Similarly, computers are quickly replaced—more than 20 million are thrown away each year in the United States. Many people buy clothes and shoes that they hardly ever wear. If a cheap garment stretches after a few washes, they throw it away. Added to this waste is all the packaging that surrounds new items, resulting in a mountain of garbage.

Packaging

Goods are packaged to keep them clean and to protect them from being damaged in transit. Packaging is also designed to make the goods look more attractive and enticing. For example, computer games, which consist of a CD-ROM, are sold in boxes that are much bigger and bulkier than the CD-ROM. DVDs come in larger plastic boxes, molded inside to fit the DVD. To help combat global warming, manufacturers should use minimal packaging, made if possible from recycled materials.

The packaging that surrounds a DVD is very bulky and may create more carbon dioxide to manufacture than the DVD itself.

Adding to global warming

Packaging is often made from plastics, which are made from oil, a fossil fuel. Plastic is light and can be manufactured into many flexible materials, including cellophane, polythene, and polystyrene. Whatever the material, however, packaging is made by machines that use electricity generated by burning fossil fuels. So, packaging may contribute more to global warming that the actual item you are buying. Once you have unwrapped your new purchase, the packaging is no longer needed and you throw it away.

These shoppers are carrying plastic bags from several different stores. Instead of accepting free plastic bags that will be thrown away, put all your shopping in one reusable bag.

BOTTLED WATER
It is very healthy to drink water, but buying water in plastic bottles, which are thrown away when they are empty, damages the environment and contributes to global warming. Each day, more than 60 million plastic water bottles are thrown away in the United States. Plastic does not rot, so most of these bottles are filling up garbage dumps. Instead of buying bottled water, it is better to buy a water filter so that you can filter your tap water instead.

Landfill sites are ugly, attract pests, and produce the greenhouse gas methane.

Disposing of waste

Waste that is not recycled (see pages 38 and 39) has to be disposed of somewhere. Most of it is flattened and buried in the ground. This is called **landfill.** Some of it is burned in **incinerators**, but they produce carbon dioxide and often poisonous fumes. Many countries have rules governing how waste can be disposed of. For example, some products, such as house paint and refrigerators, contain damaging chemicals that have to be disposed of safely. Waste is mainly a problem for the developed countries, because these are the countries that buy most consumer goods.

Landfill

Until recently, most garbage was dumped into large holes in the ground and covered with soil. Today, however, many countries are running out of places to do this. Also, landfill itself causes several problems. The garbage smells, which is unpleasant for people who live nearby, and it attracts rats and other pests. A dump also creates continual heavy traffic as garbage trucks go to and from it.

Some of the garbage rots, creating methane, a damaging greenhouse gas. At some landfill sites, the methane is collected to use as a less-polluting fuel than oil. At other sites, air and liquid are added to landfill to make it decompose more quickly. Non-recyclable plastics, however, do not rot and will remain in the landfill site for hundreds of years.

Incinerators

Incinerators are huge furnaces that burn garbage. The incinerators are very hot and need to be supplied continually with garbage. It takes a lot of energy to heat an incinerator to the high temperature it needs, and so, in some places, garbage that should be recycled is being diverted to incinerators, just to keep the furnaces going. Although some incinerators generate electricity, it is still more wasteful to burn garbage than to recycle it. Burning garbage can produce poisonous fumes that are released into the atmosphere. Many people claim that incinerators are unhealthy for people who live nearby. Like landfill sites, they generate heavy traffic from garbage trucks.

Industrial waste

Industries create huge quantities of waste—in the United States each year, 300 million scrap tires and around 8.3 billion tons of general industrial waste is produced. Like domestic waste, general industrial waste is disposed of in landfill sites or incinerators.

CUT DOWN ON WASTE

Here are a few ways to reduce waste:

- Buy fewer goods.
- Do not accept plastic bags from stores—only use reusable bags.
- When possible, choose goods that are lightly packaged.
- Reuse packaging, such as yogurt containers, whenever possible.

These cosmetics are sold with very little packaging.

Act Now!

Our desire for consumer goods is fueling global warming, using up Earth's resources, and creating huge amounts of garbage. Manufacturers can change the way they package and distribute goods. Farmers can return to more traditional farming methods, stop using so many chemicals on their crops, and treat their animals more humanely. But we cannot wait for manufacturers and farmers to change—we have to act ourselves. Why? Because global warming is happening much faster than scientists previously predicted.

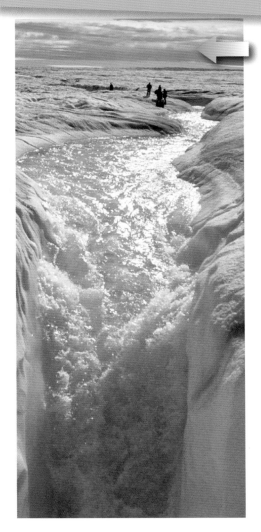

Glaciers are melting faster than scientists predicted.

Running out of time

Scientists used to think that we had several decades before the worst effects of global warming would occur. Although the average temperature of Earth has increased by less than 1.8 °F (1 °C), glaciers in the Arctic, Antarctic, and on high mountain tops are melting faster than expected. In only a few years, glaciers in Norway have retreated several hundred feet. As these glaciers melt, the water runs out the bottom and eventually into the sea. Where glaciers meet the sea, for example, in Greenland, huge chunks of ice are breaking off (called **calving**) and tipping into the sea, raising sea levels.

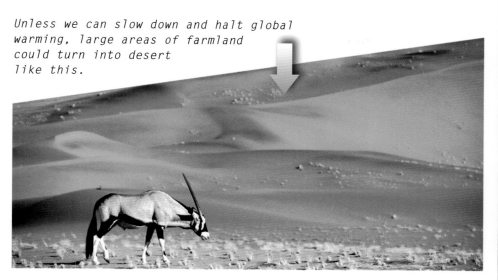

Unless we can slow down and halt global warming, large areas of farmland could turn into desert like this.

Trouble ahead

Earth absorbs about half of the billions of extra tons of carbon dioxide we produce each year, but the other half is building up in the atmosphere. Even if we stopped burning all fossil fuels now, the temperature of Earth will still rise due to the extra carbon dioxide already in the air. We have to act now to stop Earth from warming more than 3.6 °F (2 °C) altogether. If we do not, global warming could spiral out of control.

The rain forests could become so dry that they start to catch fire and eventually burn down completely. The land around the Arctic Ocean is **tundra**, a frozen swamp of partly decayed plants. As the climate warms, the tundra will begin to melt, releasing billions of tons of methane and carbon dioxide from the rotting plants. These extra gases will increase global warming still further.

Changing the way we live

The good news is that it is not too late to prevent the worst disasters that global warming will bring if things continue as they are now. Manufacturers and farmers produce masses of cheap goods and cheap food because we buy them, and the more enticing the packaging, the more we buy. Carefully choosing what we buy and what we do not buy will change the way manufacturers and farmers produce goods and sell them to us. Cutting out waste is amazingly effective—it can save up to 30 percent of carbon emissions.

Secondhand clothes can be a good value for the money. If you like vintage clothes, stores like this are a good place to look.

Buy less

Reduce, repair, reuse, and recycle—these are the four ways to reduce consumerism. Most people in developed countries have many more clothes and other things than they need or can really use. Before you buy something, stop and think about whether you really need it or are just buying it to make yourself feel good. How many T-shirts or shoes do you actually need? When you do buy something, do not necessarily buy the cheapest option—cheap things often do not last long. Look instead for things that are well made from materials that can be recycled and by people who were paid fair wages.

Repair

When something breaks down, see if you can get it repaired. It is cheaper to repair shoes, for example, than to buy new ones. Electrical goods can often be repaired. If the item was so cheap it is not worth repairing, think about buying a better quality one next time.

Reuse

Many items can be reused when you have finished with them, particularly clothes, shoes, CDs, books, DVDs, and CD-ROMs. Provided your clothes are in good condition, you can take them to a charity store. Someone else can get more wear out of them, and the money raised will help people in need. Charity stores and secondhand clothes stores are good places to look for clothes to buy. You can often find good-quality clothes being sold for cheap prices. You can also buy and sell secondhand goods on auction websites such as eBay.

Eat less meat

You do not have to be totally vegetarian to eat less meat. Too much red meat can be unhealthy, and cows take up valuable land that could be used to grow food crops. They also produce huge amounts of methane, a gas that is produced by their digestive systems. Nearly one-fifth of all the methane in the air is produced by farm animals! (Methane traps 20 times as much heat as the same weight of carbon dioxide.)

SHOPPING CHECKLIST

- Only buy new things you really need.
- Only buy things that will last. Do not buy things that soon break down or wear out.
- Look for clothes made from organic cotton.
- When something breaks down, see if it can be repaired.
- Reuse gift wrapping, envelopes, and everything else you can.
- Look for energy efficiency labels.
- Look to see where the item was made. Use the Internet to find out which companies have a good employment record and which have a bad record.

Vegetarian food is usually healthy and better for the environment.

The energy saved by recycling a single bottle could power a computer for 30 minutes.

Recycle

If you cannot repair or reuse things you no longer want, then recycle them if possible. Things made of paper, glass, metal, and plastic can all be recycled. This means that the material they are made of is used again and so saves Earth's resources. It also keeps them out of landfill sites. Manufacturing goods from recycled materials does take energy, but not as much as making them from scratch.

Recycling centers

Many cities collect items to be recycled from your home, or you can sort them into special bins for different materials—for example, paper, cardboard, glass of different colors, metals, and plastics. Electronic goods should be recycled to reclaim the parts of them that can be reused.

RECYCLING PAPER
Each ton of paper that is recycled can save:
- 17 trees
- 400 gallons of oil
- 7,000 gallons of water
- 3 cubic yards of landfill.

To make recycling more efficient, you should wash out bottles and cans first and not mix in unwanted things, such as plastic wrappers, with the newspapers. Not all plastic things can be recycled—check whether it has a recycling symbol.

BUY RECYCLED GOODS

In addition to recycling unwanted things, look for things that are made of recycled materials when you buy something new. Cards and wrapping paper, for example, are often printed on recycled paper.

Saving resources

Recycling saves raw materials and some energy. Paper is mixed with water to make pulp, instead of cutting down trees to pulp their wood. While new glass is made by heating quartz or silica to a very high temperature, old glass can be melted down at much lower temperatures. It takes 20 times more energy to make a new aluminium can than to recycle a used one. Food scraps and peelings are made into compost, which is full of nutrients and avoids using chemical fertilizers.

Making recycling carbon-free

Although recycling saves resources, it does use energy. This is why it is better to reuse and repair rather than recycle. Recycling adds to global warming if it uses electricity that has been generated at a power station that burns fossil fuels. Electricity that has been generated by wind turbines or **solar power** creates much less carbon dioxide.

These glass beads are made of recycled glass.

Look beyond the label

Companies that sell designer labels want you to believe that when you buy their clothes, you are buying into a whole way of life. They want you to feel cool, up-to-the-minute, and like someone to be respected, but, of course, all you are actually buying is a pair of sneakers or an item of clothing. Designer labels are expensive because so much money is spent on advertising them. If you look beyond the label, you will often find that the way the company's goods are produced is often not cool or fair. Their factories are usually in developing countries. The workers have to labor long hours in unhealthy conditions and are paid wages so low they can scarcely feed their families. There is an alternative—it is called **fair trade**.

Fair trade

Fair trade is a system that ensures that the people who produce a crop or work in a factory are paid a fair amount. The extra they are paid makes a big difference to them, but only adds a small amount to the price we pay. Many fair trade agreements are for food crops, such as chocolate, coffee, and bananas. The workers who benefit from them often work together in village **cooperatives.** This means that they share the work and the money they receive equally. They often use some of the profits to benefit the whole village by investing in clean water, schools, and medical care.

These are the logos to look for! You will see them on fair trade products, meaning on products where the people who produce them have been fairly paid.

Problems with fair trade

Many people do not want to buy goods that exploit people in developing countries, and so they are eager to buy fair trade goods instead. Even large companies are beginning to offer fair trade goods, which is good news—but be careful. Some companies label their products fair trade when only part of the process qualifies for the label. For example, a garment may be labeled fair trade because the cotton was produced under a fair trade agreement, although the garment itself was made in a **sweatshop** in Bangladesh.

Many café chains include a fair trade option on their menu— but should all the options be fair trade?

41

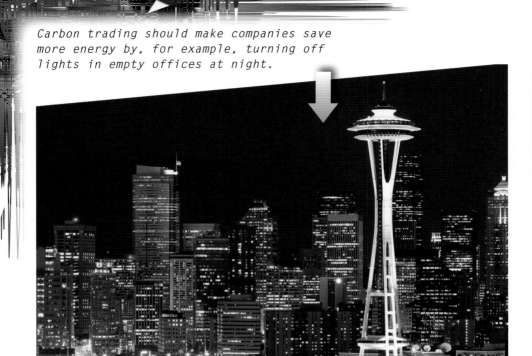

Carbon trading should make companies save more energy by, for example, turning off lights in empty offices at night.

The bigger picture

You can influence companies by what you do and do not buy, and you can help to slow down global warming by buying fewer new things and by reusing, repairing, and recycling old things. But you need to think wider than that. Try to persuade your friends to change the way they shop and dispose of garbage, too. Does your school recycle trash, for example? Does it waste resources? Schools use far more energy than a single family, and big companies with many offices use more energy still.

Carbon trading

In 2006 the world's people were producing around 77 billion tons of carbon dioxide—twice as much as Earth can absorb. If countries agreed, they could calculate how much carbon dioxide each could safely emit to cut the total by half. Then, within a country, each large company and institution, such as hospitals, schools, and government offices, could be allowed to emit a safe amount of carbon dioxide. This is part of the idea behind **carbon trading**.

In carbon trading, large companies are each allocated a certain amount of carbon dioxide. If a company exceeds its permitted amount, it can buy extra allowances from companies that have emitted less. In this way "clean" companies make money. Some European countries are trying this idea, but it will only work if the permitted amounts are set low enough. The danger is that the biggest and most polluting companies will simply carry on as they are instead of reducing their pollution.

China and India

The countries that create most greenhouse gases per head are the developed industrialized countries in North America, Europe, and Australia. These countries need to reduce their carbon dioxide emissions by more than half, because developing countries will emit more as they become industrialized, too. China and India are industrializing fast, and their carbon dioxide emissions are increasing. If countries agree to set limits, they need to take into account that much of the carbon dioxide developing countries emit is from factories and farms that are producing goods and crops for the developed countries.

These toys are made from soft-drink cans. People in developing countries are good at reusing materials to make new objects.

Glossary

air-freight
transporting goods by airplane

antibiotics medicines that kill bacteria

calving way a glacier produces icebergs as the end of the glacier breaks off and falls into the sea

carbon dioxide gas that is found mainly in the atmosphere

carbon trading system whereby companies and/or countries are each allocated a weight of carbon (meaning carbon dioxide) they can produce. Companies or countries that produce more than their allocation buy extra allowances from companies or countries that produce less than their allocation.

chlorofluorocarbons chlorofluorcarbons (also known as CFCs) are used in refrigerators and other products. When they are released into the air, they become greenhouse gases and damage the ozone layer.

climate change change in the usual patterns of climate

cooperative organization whose members own the business

crop rotation system of farming in which different crops are grown in each field each year

developed country nation, such as the United States or Australia, with a high standard of living due to its advanced economy

developing country nation, such as Kenya or India, where most people rely on farming and are poorer than those in developed nations

drought unusual shortage of rain

emission release of waste substances into the environment, particularly into the atmosphere, rivers, or the sea

factory farming system of farming that mass-produces animals and crops, usually using chemicals and other intensive methods of farming

fair trade trade that is overseen by organizations to make sure that it is fair. This means that goods are bought from producers at a fair price—one that provides an income on which workers can survive.

fertilizer substance that gives plants the nutrients they need to grow well

fossil fuels coal, oil, and natural gas. These fuels are called fossil fuels because they formed millions of years ago.

free-range system of farming animals in which the animals are given space to move around

gene part of living cells that is passed from parents to offspring and determines the biological make-up of the offspring

genetic modification scientific process in which the genes from one species are introduced into a different species

global warming increase in the average temperature of the surface of Earth

greenhouse gas gas in the atmosphere that traps the Sun's heat and thus leads to global warming

herbicide chemical poison used to kill unwanted plants

hormone chemical produced by a plant or animal that helps to control how the plant or animal functions

hurricane very severe storm involving strong winds over 74 mph (118 kph) and heavy rain

incinerator furnace for burning things such as waste

intensively produced crop crop that is grown year after year on the same land with the help of fertilizers and other chemicals

landfill way of disposing of garbage by burying it in deep holes in the ground

methane natural gas and one of the greenhouse gases

minimum wage lowest rate of pay that it is legal to pay in a particular country

monoculture system of farming in which only one crop is grown year after year

nitrous oxide one of the greenhouse gases, mostly produced through farming

organic farming method of farming that uses antiobiotics only when necessary and minimal or no artificial fertilizers or other chemicals

pesticide poison that kills pests, particularly those that attack crops

photosynthesis process in which carbon dioxide from the air and water is combined using chlorophyll and the energy of sunlight to produce sugar. Photosynthesis produces oxygen as a waste gas.

power station building or complex of devices that generates large amounts of electricity

rain forest forest that grows in warm, wet areas of the world. Most rain forest grows in the tropics and contains millions of different species of plants and animals.

refinery building in which oil is refined, or separated, into different substances

regulated controlled

selective breeding breeding farm animals to produce preferred characteristics

solar power using the energy of sunlight or the heat of the Sun to generate electricity

sweatshop clothes factory in which the workers are paid very low wages

synthetic material material, such as plastic, nylon, and acrylic, that is made from oil

terminator seed seed that has been genetically modified so that the plants it grows into do not produce fertile seeds that can be used to grow more plants the following year

tundra treeless area of land that borders the Arctic and is also found just below the permanent snows of high mountains

turbine device that rotates to generate electricity

typhoon name given to a hurricane in Southeast Asia

United Nations (UN) international organization to which most countries belong. The United Nations aims to promote cooperation among nations to encourage economic development and maintain peace.

yield output that is harvested

Further Information

Some websites give information about specific topics. Other websites give information about many aspects of global warming, its consequences, and what you can do. This is a selection of both kinds of websites:

Global warming

www.epa.gov/climatechange/
Website of the U.S. Environmental Protection Agency, which explains global warming and its effect on the environment and ecosystems and suggests various things you can do.

www.wri.org/climate/topic_data_trends.cfm
Website of the World Resources Institute, which gives a world map in which the area of each country is in proportion to the weight of carbon dioxide it emits.

www.energyquest.ca.gov/story/chapter08.html
Energy Quest, a website of the California Energy Commission, explains how coal, oil, and natural gas were formed.

www.commondreams.org/headlines06/0312-03.htm
Gives an article about tipping points in the Arctic and how they will accelerate global warming.

www.climatehotmap.org/
A website that gives a map showing early warning signs of global warming in different continents. Produced by several organizations, including World Resources Institute, Environmental Defense, and World Wildlife Fund.

www.earthinstitute.columbia.edu/crosscutting/climate.html
Website of the Earth Institute at Columbia University in New York City, it outlines the consequences of global warming and suggests some things you can do.

www.greenpeace.org/usa/campaigns/global-warming-and-energy
Website of environmental campaigning organization Greenpeace, with facts and predictions concerning global warming and energy.

www.sierraclub.org/globalwarming/qa/
Website of the Sierra Club, covering global warming and things you can do about it.

www.climatecrisis.net/
Website for the movie *An Inconvenient Truth*, which includes facts about global warming and things you can do.

MAKING THE OCEAN BLOOM

Australian scientist Ian Jones has discovered that adding a fertilizer to the oceans increases the number of phytoplankton—the microscopic plants that feed the oceans' food chains. Like land plants, they absorb carbon dioxide from the air and, when they die, they sink to the bottom of the ocean, taking the carbon dioxide with them. The best fertilizer he has found is urea—one of the ingredients of urine!

Cotton

www.stepin.org/casestudy.php?id=ecofashion&page=9
Educational website comparing organic cotton and cotton grown with pesticides.

Food and fossil fuel

www.ecoliteracy.org/publications/rsl/tom-starrs.html
Tells you about fossil fuel and how you can choose your food to reduce the amount of carbon dioxide.

Organic farming

www.soilassociation.org/web/sa/saweb.nsf/living/index.html
Website of the Soil Association, an organization that campaigns for organic farming, giving you reasons to buy organic products.

www.newscientist.com/article.ns?id=dn6496
Article from the New Scientist magazine about how organic farming helps diversity.

Hydrogen fuel

www.hydrogen.co.uk/h2/hydrogen.htm
Gives diagram showing how hydrogen could be produced from renewable sources of electricity and used to power buildings and transportation.

www.fctec.com/fctec_types_pem.asp
Website of the U.S. Department of Defense Fuel Cell Test and Evaluation Center. This tells you about how a hydrogen fuel cell works. The proton exchange membrane fuel cell (PEM) is the best kind of hydrogen fuel cell for buildings.

Carbon offsetting

www.carbonfootprint.com/USA/calculator.html
Website that allows you to calculate how much carbon your family produces.

*I*ndex